# BETWEEN SHADOWS & STARLIGHTS

## A COLLECTION OF HYPOTHETICAL REALITIES & DREAMSCAPES

SAMARTH RAJ TOMAR

Made with ♥ on the Notion Press Platform
www.notionpress.com

*To Dadi and Dadu,*

*Your love and wisdom remain in my soul, and though you're watching from above, every word in this book is a piece of my heart, forever dedicated to you.*

# Contents

# Contents

# Foreword

*"To those who dare to see not just the world as it is, but as it could be!"*

Some stories are never spoken, some dreams are never lived, and some colors are never named. They exist in the spaces between words, in the hush of forgotten pages, in the echoes of what was left unsaid. *Between the Shadows & Starlight* is a journey into these unseen realms, a collection of poetry that dares to explore what lingers in the corners of our minds and hearts.

Samarth Raj Tomar invites you to step beyond the ordinary—to question, to feel, and to imagine. This book is not just about dreams; it is about their longing, about love that lingers but never stays, about silence that aches to be heard, and about the weight of unspoken emotions that shape who we become.

Perhaps, within these pages, you will find your own forgotten thoughts staring back at you. Perhaps, between the lines, you will discover words you didn't even know you were searching for. Let this book be more than poetry—let it be a mirror to your own soul, a place where the unimagined finally finds a voice.

# Preface

Poetry is not just written—it is felt, lived, and breathed. It is the quiet sigh in the night, the ache of an unspoken word, the warmth of a memory that refuses to fade. *Between the Shadows & Starlight* was never meant to be just a collection of poems; it is a journey through the lost, the unsaid, and the deeply imagined.

From chasing forgotten words to embracing the silence they leave behind, from longing for love to understanding its fleeting nature, this book carries the emotions we often push aside. It is a reflection of every moment that lingers in the heart, every thought that was never voiced, and every dream that fades before morning.

If you have ever felt the weight of a love that never found its home, if you have ever searched for meaning in the quiet spaces of your own mind—this book is for you. It belongs to every heart that has dared to dream beyond the limits of reality. May these words find you in the silence and make you feel a little less alone.

Acknowledgements

Gratitude is a feeling too vast to be contained in words, yet here I try.

First and foremost, I thank God for blessing me with the ability to see beyond what exists, to dream of worlds unseen, and to pour them onto paper. Without this gift, this book would have remained just another echo in my mind, lost in the silence of the unwritten.

To my grandparents—your love is the quiet strength that holds me up. It shines through every bright day and lingers in the darkest nights, reminding me that I am never alone. Your presence, whether near or far, is the warmth that fuels my dreams.

To my parents, my guiding angels—you have been my light, my foundation, and my unwavering support. Your belief in me, your encouragement in both my successes and failures, and your sacrifices have given me the courage to chase my dreams. Without your support, both emotionally and financially, this book might have remained just a thought. Every word in these pages carries a part of your love.

To my sister, my rock—you have been my constant, my safe place, my biggest inspiration. Your care, your wisdom, and the way you silently uplift everyone around you amaze me every day. You have taught me to think beyond the ordinary, to embrace the unknown, and to find beauty in the unexpected. This book exists because you have always believed in me, even when I doubted myself.

To my friends—Harsh, for designing a cover that breathes life into my words, Yug and Palak, for standing beside me with unwavering support and honest reviews. Your faith in me, your encouragement, and your patience have been my strength. This journey would not have been the same without you all.

And finally, to you—the reader. You have chosen to walk through these pages, to enter my world of imagination, emotions, and unspoken truths. Thank you for trusting me with your time, your thoughts, and your heart. I hope this book resonates with you, that it stirs something deep within, and that it gives you the same thrill I felt while writing it.

This book is not just mine; it belongs to every soul who dares to dream beyond reality.

# Prologue

***Stories Once Locked Away….***

*Today, by soaking these empty pages in my ink so deep,*
*I long to feel their silence rise and speak...*
*So I thought, why not write again today,*
*And give words to the sorrow that quietness conveys!*
*So here I am, back once more,*
*With the same old tales from my heart's very core,*
*Stories once locked in a chest so tight,*
*Buried away from the world's sight...*
*Yet, when I opened that book today,*
*These very words met my gaze in the very first way!*
*So now you must know—*
*This is something new yet old,*
*Not from the present, but not from days of old…*
*A story untold!*
*A story so close to my heart,*
*A story that played its writer's part,*
*But no one was there to read from the start!*
*And now,*
*The time has come, the wait is through,*
*This tale has found its listeners too!*

*Aaj inn khali kore panno ko apni kalam ki siyahi se bhigo kar, inke ultepan par kuch ubhrapan mehsoos karne ki chah hui hai… Socha, aaj phir se kuch likh kar ghum-e-khamoshiyon ko alfaaz diye jaaye! To lo, aa gaya main wapas! Apni*

*unhi daastan ke saath, jo kabhi kahin kisi dil-e-sadooq mein dabakar qaid kar di gayi thi... Halaanki, jab khola woh bachcha, to sabse upar inse hi aankhein ru-ba-ru hui! To ab jaan lo—yeh kuch nayi si purani, filhal ki nahi, par arson purani bhi nahi... Kuch aisi kahani hai! Kahani jo mere dil ke bohot kareeb hai, Kahani jisko likhne wala mila, Par kahani jisko padhne wala koi na mila! Aur ab, Iss kahani ko sunne waalon ki numaish mil gayi!*

*There are places where stories go when they are forgotten. Words left unsaid, dreams abandoned at the edge of sleep, colors that never found their name. I have wandered through these places, searching for the echoes of something unspoken. Tonight, I open the first door.*

# 1. The Library of Lost Souls

Today, once again, in the city of books, I arrived,
In those little alleys, my heart took a stride.
Between those towering buildings so high,
Seeing a few windows, a journey revived.
Today, once again, in the city of books, I arrived!
The rustling of pages so slight,
The shelves creaking open quiet,
The ticking clock in steady chime,
And sirens wailing from outside!
Hearing them again, my heart smiled bright!
Today, once again, in the city of books, I arrived!
"Silence Please," "No Smoking," "You are under CCTV surveillance,"
Reading them once more, it felt like confinement in existence!
Seeing the shelves of colorful spines,
An old desire awoke inside!
Today, once again, in the city of books, I arrived!
Those long and endless wooden desks,
With scattered books on them left,
Books that someone once read and forgot,
Books that never found their slot,
Books that longed for a gentle embrace,
Books that stayed quiet, in silent space!
Watching them yearn, a vision revived,
Today, once again, in the city of books, I arrived!

Some restless whispers in my mind,
Some wishes to stay behind,
Some quiet despair locked inside,
Yet all they said as I turned away—
"I don't feel like staying today!"
Just an excuse, a fleeting guise,
And now, from this city, it's time to say goodbye!

*Aaj phir unn kitaabon ke sheher mein mera aana hua,*
*Unn chhoti-chhoti galiyon mein dil ko tehlana hua.*
*Unn unchi-unchi imaarton ke beech,*
*Chand khidkiyon ko dekh ek safar purana hua.*
*Aaj phir unn kitaabon ke sheher mein mera aana hua!*
*Unn panno ki fadfadahat,*
*Unn almariyon ki dheere se khulti awaaz,*
*Uss ghadi ki tik-tik,*
*Aur uss khidki ke bahar se aati siren ki awaaz!*
*Aaj phir unko sunkar dil ka muskurana hua!*
*Aaj phir iss kitaabon ke sheher mein mera aana hua!*
*"Silence Please", "No Smoking", "You are under CCTV surveillance"*
*Padhkar phir ek baar aisa laga,*
*Jaise kisi bandish mein rahe zamana hua!*
*Unn rangin panno ke khaane ko dekh,*
*Aisa laga jaise unko tatolne ek jazba purana hua!*
*Aaj phir iss kitaabon ke sheher mein mera aana hua!*
*Woh lambi-lambi chaupaayi maizien,*
*Woh unpar bikhri kuch chand kitaabein,*
*Kitaabein jo shayad kisi ne istemaal karke chhod di!*

*Kitaabein jo shayad apni jagah unn khaanon mein na bana payin!*
*Kitaabein jo bechain thi kisi ke sparsh ke liye!*
*Kitaabein jo kuch bol na payin!*
*Unn kitaabon ko tadapta dekh,*
*Ek manzar purana hua!*
*Aaj phir iss kitaabon ke sheher mein mera aana hua!*
*Kuch bechain mann ki bhasha,*
*Kuch yahan tham jaane ki aasha,*
*Kuch dil mein dab rahi ashaant nirasha,*
*Bas jaane ke liye keh rahi thi,*
*"Mann nahi lag raha yahan!"*
*Yeh toh bas ek bahana hua,*
*Aur ab iss sheher se phir mera jaana hua!*

*As I walked through the hushed corridors of forgotten stories, I wondered—what happens to the words that were never written? Do they echo in the sleepless corners of the mind, waiting for someone to dream them into existence?*

## 2. Echoes of a Sleepless Mind

What is a Dream?
A bird with colors never seen before,
Gliding across a sky of endless shore.
A whisper of wind in the silent night,
A flicker of hope in a lost man's fight.
Is it a star that waits to be found,
Or the echo of wishes, soft yet profound?
Is it a child who leaps and flies,
Or an artist lost in his painted skies?
That dress you saved for a perfect day,
The melody in a song that never fades away.
The footsteps on roads untold,
The warmth of hands you long to hold.
What is a dream?
A lover's letter sealed with time,
A poet's rhythm lost in rhyme.
A sailor's faith in waves so deep,
Or a mother's prayer when her baby sleeps.
Is it a thought that won't let you rest,
Or the heart that beats within your chest?
Is it the past that calls your name,
Or the future waiting to play its game?
A dream is fragile, yet strong as steel,
It's what you chase, what you feel.
A spark, a fire, a silent scream,

A world unseen—**that is a dream.**

*But dreams are not just whispers; they are hues of longing, fragments of the unknown. What if the colors that defined our world could change? What if the deepest darkness was not dark enough to hold the weight of our imagination?*

# 3. What if the color was darker than black?

The red blood may provoke less passion.
The Yellow might shine less joy in action.
The green may breathe less satisfaction.
The blue might gaze an uneasy depression.
And so the men with black shirts might play havoc with fashion!
What if the color was darker than black?
The Voilet may loose its majesty.
The Indigo may grow more mystery.
The orange might devoid its geniality.
The grey lays waste to it's authority!
And so the shadows might fade into obscurity!
What if the color was darker than black?
The black nights might go!
The dark thoughts might not say you a dreamy hello!
You shall sleep tight under your pillow!
And maybe there is no black heart ? in your bio!
And so you might have more facial glow!
What if the color was darker than black?
Maybe the steepy chessboard shall not go to knuckle.
Maybe there are no hard feels between kith and kin to battle.
Maybe the black child borns more pretty.
Maybe we wear black when we pray our deity.
And so the world might look more fancy!
And so I need a color darker than black!

And so i need a color darker than black!

*I searched for this new shade, for a depth beyond black—one that could rewrite the meaning of shadows. But in chasing the unknown, I found myself questioning—what if the world was never meant to see beyond what it already fears?*

# 4. Beyond the Dark 2.0

**What if a color was darker than black?**
Would the night lose its endless track?
Would the stars still dare to shine,
Or fade into a shade divine?
Would red still rage with burning fire,
Or turn to embers, lost, expired?
Would yellow dance in golden streams,
Or dim like dying candle dreams?
Would green still whisper peace and cheer,
Or wilt away in silent fear?
Would blue still paint the endless deep,
Or drown in tides too dark to keep?
**What if a color was darker than black?**
Would shadows cease to leave a trace?
Would fear no longer wear its face?
Would thoughts once lost in midnight's hue,
Now glow in shades of something new?
Would violet still hold royal grace,
Or sink into a voided space?
Would orange warm the autumn air,
Or vanish, leaving colors bare?
**What if a color was darker than black?**
Would night be day, and day be night?
Would dreams lose form, dissolve from sight?
Would echoes fade where silence grew,

And time stand still in shades untrue?
Would chessboards blur in endless gray?
Would conflict lose its bitter play?
Would hearts once heavy, weighed in sorrow,
Find a brighter shade tomorrow?
And so I ask, both bold and free,
A world much darker—could it be?
A shade unseen, beyond the track,
I need a color darker than black.

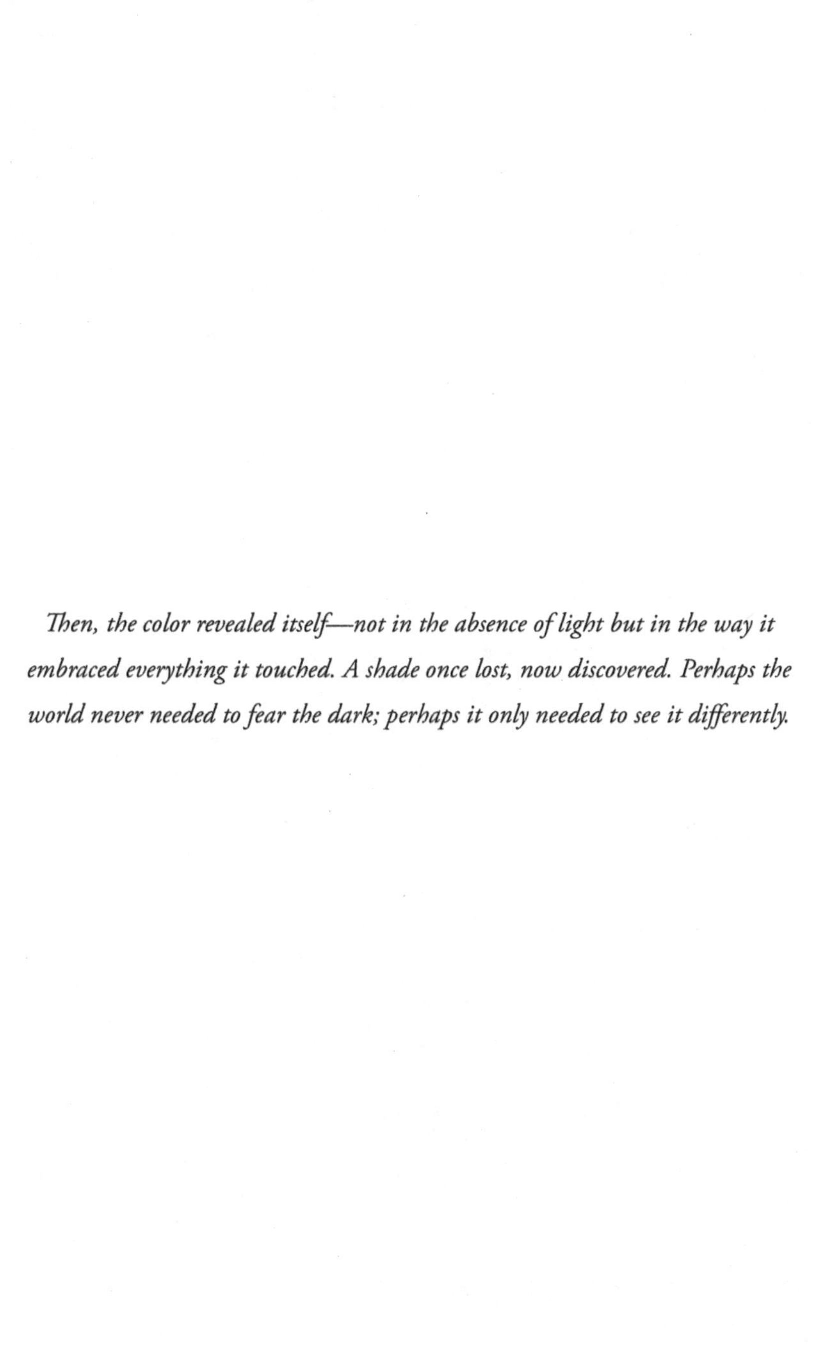

*Then, the color revealed itself—not in the absence of light but in the way it embraced everything it touched. A shade once lost, now discovered. Perhaps the world never needed to fear the dark; perhaps it only needed to see it differently.*

# 5. A Shade Discovered!

**Once, we feared the night so deep,**
A place where silent shadows creep.
But now we see, beyond the track,
A shade once lost—darker than black.
The **child once named in whispered tone,**
Now shines in hues that match his own.
His beauty bold, his laughter bright,
Not judged by darkness, but by light.
The **robes once banned in sacred space,**
Now grace the temple's holy place.
No color cursed, no shade denied,
For faith and hues now walk allied.
The **chessboard gleams, its pattern new,**
No longer stark in black and blue.
The war of minds, the bitter play,
Now softened into subtle grey.
The **nights no longer bring despair,**
But wrap us in their velvet care.
A deeper dark, yet full of peace,
Where haunted thoughts now find release.
And in this world, so bright, so vast,
The wounds of time have healed at last.
A darker black, a deeper shade,
Yet fear and sorrow start to fade.

So let it shine, this unknown hue,
A world reborn, in colors true.
No shade too dark, no light too bright,
Just harmony—a perfect sight.

*But what are colors if not reflections of the moments we lose? Time, too, holds shades of its own—fading loves, unsaid words, and destinies that slip through our grasp like forgotten ink on old parchment.*

# 6. Bound by Fate ; Lost in Time

The sun scorched your hunt that day,
I longed for words, yet none could stay.
Love was slipping, turning to hate,
As if bound by an unkind fate.
I searched for you in empty air,
The moon refused its silver glare.
Drifting high in love's embrace,
Now cut adrift—a lost kite's trace.
The morning came, a hollow sigh,
I woke beneath a vacant sky.
And as I thought of all I'd say,
It was a dream that keeps me away.
Yet echoes linger, soft and slow,
A haunting tune I used to know.
Was it love, or was it pain?
Or just a storm that left no rain?

*And just like that, love became a dream—one that returned every night but never stayed till morning. Some dreams are meant to be lived, others to be lost. But the cruelest ones? They are the ones that haunt us in silence.*

# 7. A Dream That Never Woke!

**Today felt like a lovely day!**
Yet I had to hide from you the storm inside that swayed.
Why did you do this, tell me why?
Why did you make my heart cry?
This crazy soul had so much to say,
To lose itself in you, to drift away...
But this foolish heart was bound to break,
Left to drown in sorrow's wake!
**Today, I saw you,**
Saw your face, so torn and blue.
I watched your hair dance in the breeze,
And in that moment, I felt at ease...
Then my eyes fell upon your hands,
Held so tightly within his clasp…
Your joy was clear, your smile so bright,
But, I swear to you, in that moment, I died!
**You pulled me close, into your embrace!**
Perhaps you didn't want to, yet gave me that place...
Yes, I was nothing, just a fleeting haze,
Still, for a moment, you called me yours in a daze!
I don't know why,
But swallowing the pain, one more time,
I hugged you back,
Like you were still mine!

**Do you remember?**
We both wore the same attire that day!
Yet, between us, there was one difference to say.
Your white-checkered dupatta so bright,
Had no trace of the color black in sight!
Perhaps you wanted me to believe,
That you had nothing left to deceive...
That in this white so pure and free,
No hidden truths could ever be seen!
**But you forgot—**
I had already seen the shade you tried to hide!
No matter how much you tucked it inside,
That darkness you buried deep away,
Has left my nights in disarray!
Your veil of white revealed it all,
That silence is now my heart's call...
So in search of peace, in search of rest,
I lay my head upon your chest!
**Yet sleep refused to settle in...**
Yes, deep inside, my eyes were dim!
Lost in thought, I searched for me,
Even beneath the scattered trees...
And through the golden rays that seeped,
Your hands still held a touch so deep!
**With love, or perhaps in silent pain,**
You ran your fingers through my tangled mane...
And my restless strands in your hold,
Begged you softly, to not let go!
Beneath your veil, I heard a sound,

The words my restless soul had found!
**Yet, you couldn't hear…**
Perhaps you were never meant to be near!
Now I gather myself, piece by piece,
Holding on to your words, your memories,
Trying to teach myself somehow,
To face these dark, unknown nights now!

*In silence, I sought refuge in words. But words are never just ink on a page; they are confessions. And when you pour your heart onto paper, do you heal—or do you leave another scar behind?*

# 8. Ink - Stained Confessions

The kid inside me found a spark,
When the Almighty gifted me you…
The life before you survived in the dark,
I thought I'd tell none but you…
The excitement rose to the ninth cloud!
My inner soul was happy and loud!
At first, I treated you like a humanoid…
But then, a night came, and everything was destroyed!
The foolish me...
As soon as I opened you,
I rushed my pen to write on you!
That night, I wanted to fill every page…
Forgot to keep my head calm—my hands had rage!
My eyes saw your condition was terrible...
My ears heard stories, sharable...
But the selfish me,
Forgot to ask what *you* had been through,
Before I started to scribble!
The tip of my pen held sharpness untold,
I started writing my pain in bold…
I cut you deeper,
Left you with scars unhidden,
I talked loud and spilled my mind,
For hours and hours, unbidden!

You screamed for rest,
Yet, the crazy me forgot—you needed to be at your best!
You gave me signals, a silent request,
But I thought I was the saddest…
I still wrote—cut—tore your page,
As if you'd find another stage…
You warned me hard, not to tear you apart…
Maybe the ruckus of the past needed an early start!
Now, since I have no empty page to write,
I see that what I did wasn't right!
I poured out the mess in my head,
Only to realize I missed the *important* unsaid…
I disrespected you with my glare…
And now I question—how did I dare?
Oh, God, You gifted me something precious and rare…
I regret—I should have handled it with care.
Maybe now, I won't forgive myself…
Maybe now, I can't hide her in my bookshelf…
I should have given a warmer quilt…
Maybe now, I'm left with nothing but guilt…
The excitement inside me wanted to make it divine…
Look! The immature me—
I forgot to write my name,
Before I could rhyme…

*But some words never find their way out. They linger in the spaces between conversations, threading themselves into our very being—until one day, they become a language only we understand.*

# 9. Threads of the Unspoken

My clothes won't tell you the story I wear,
Now it's just life in another gear.
There's something unknown in today's air...
Maybe that's why people keep saying—
*"That's not fair!"*
It is beautiful,
It's aesthetic,
Sometimes, it feels like life,
And sometimes, pathetic.
I am silent,
Not because I'm tense.
I don't become violent,
Though my rage is intense.
You keep me in the dark,
I won't let you spark.
It's as simple as a shark—
You can't find one in a water park.

*Some words remain locked beneath the skin, woven into the fabric of silence, unheard yet aching to be known. But when silence is mistaken for pride, when unspoken pain is called ego, the world becomes a mirror that reflects blame instead of understanding. And so, I wore their accusations like a second skin, wondering—was it ever truly my fault?*

# 10. EGO! - 'The Blame that was never Mine.'

It was MY EGO to them,
It was the pressure on me.
- Work went unwilling which was willingly did by me.
It was MY EGO to them,
It was the deadline to me.
- I postponed the plans which were always made prior by me.
It was MY EGO to them,
It was their respect to me.
- I heard the unheard and kept it inside me.
It was MY EGO to them,
It was their minacity to me.
- I still did their will that's what others never know still.
It was MY EGO to them,
It became self respect to me.
- They still pretend to kick me off when I left them untouched of me.
It was MY EGO to them,
It was Care to me.
- I still thought of them and they made it about me.
It was MY EGO to them,
It was Helplessness to me.
- I was made to do so and they thought i did it by me.
It was MY EGO to them,
It was never a one for me.
- I could've came back but Thanks to Me.

Coz Still,
It is MY EGO to them.
And That's not the real me!

*The weight of blame is a lonely thing. It drives you to places where no apology can reach, where conversations become whispers of the past. I sat there, across from ghosts of what once was, stirring the memories in my glass, wondering—was it loneliness that found me, or had I chosen it long before?*

# 11. A Table for One!

Sitting inside a café,
Talking to myself about life.
Not watching the buffet,
But feeling a hunger to survive.
Me and my thoughts bath in the vibes—
The slow music, the dim lights,
The people chirping,
But I'm quiet.
I'm quiet because
I don't fight.
I don't bicker like that couple,
I don't clash in a vocal shuffle,
I don't flicker like those restless lights.
I'm alone,
Alone in those slippers tonight.
Snapping my date-life with mojitos,
Stalking my date—
Once, she was.
Reading those *"Love you to the moon and back"* quotes,
Satisfying my life's chaos.
That's all it was.
That's all it was.

*The table was never set for two. Maybe it never was. Some nights, I let the silence dine with me, pretending it didn't taste like regret. But memories are impatient guests; they don't wait to be invited. They slip into your breath, into the quiet sighs between sips of coffee, reminding you of all the yesterdays you tried to forget.*

# 12. The Breathe of Forgotten Days

With a little snort and wake-up alarm,
I welcomed the morning with open arm.
Stressed a little to have some calm,
The face had wrinkles without a charm.
Looked in the mirror... my mind noticed the eyes' error,
The spark that once glowed now buried in terror.
My breath, heavy, labored, torn,
Like a man who's seen all hope worn.
The morning coughs, like an old man's sigh,
A tremor in his chest, wondering why.
Once, my heart beat to the rhythm of love,
A wife by my side, dreams soaring above.
Now, her absence robs me of my fight,
The world feels darker with no guiding light.
The love I taught to the youth of today,
Now mocked, forgotten, lost in dismay.
They laugh at me, the Gen-Z brigade,
While I watch the pieces of my world fade.
They share their sympathy, fleeting and cold,
But tomorrow, they'll forget the tales I've told.
The house is too dark, too silent, too still,
As I breathe alone, against my will.
My lungs are starved for breath and for grace,
But I live in a hollow, forgotten place.

Once, I was whole, full of life and of dreams,
Now, all that remains are fractured seams.
I gave them love, I gave them all,
But in my solitude, I hear only the fall.
The world moves forward, indifferent to pain,
While I'm left to weather the storm of disdain.
Today, I cough like an old man lost—
A soul aching, but at what cost?
Tomorrow, my breath may fade with the day,
But the world will carry on, in its own cruel way.
No empathy left when the day turns to night,
Just shadows that linger, out of sight.

*The past lingers in the breath of forgotten days, whispering stories we try to silence. But silence knows its way home. It finds you in the dead of night, in the spaces between heartbeats, and calls you by name. And when silence speaks, do we answer, or do we run from the voice that knows us best?*

# 13. When Silence speaks my Name!

One day, I want to wake up as dead...
And maybe then, they'll say what's unsaid...
Perhaps my struggles will find their grace,
And my soul will hear the satisfaction in place.
The satisfaction I couldn't give on my last day,
The satisfaction that could have made me stay...
The satisfaction my body pretends as it lies,
The satisfaction they feel as their final prayer flies.
It'll be a day full of sorrow and strain,
Some will console the widow's pain...
Some will look through the mirror's deep trance,
Some will prepare my last resting stance...
And some will skip their bread, in mournful trance.
They'll lay me upon the bier...
Searching for my teddy bear, dear...
Offering their tears, their sorrow sincere,
Words that now I can never hear...
My final rites will be held with pride,
Four strong shoulders will carry me wide...
To the cemetery, so cold and grim,
Where fire will burn me, my life's dim.
Soon, I'll turn to ashes, no more gleam,
No one will recall my fleeting dream...
Some will return with no hair, no mustaches,

And quickly rush to the beer bashes...
As they reach home, silence will creep,
Maybe one or two will moan and weep...
But in a few days, life will move on,
A little stronger, but I'll be gone.
Maybe another life will begin to grow,
While I'm forgotten, the cycle to flow.
From above, I'll laugh at their shifting love,
Watching them move on, as if they've had enough...
They'll go on with their lives, never looking back,
Except for my picture, with the death date intact.
What use is it now, this fleeting memory?
So...
Nothing left to mourn, no more reverie...
Just...
Thank you for the formal ciao...
Thank you for the formal ciao...

*And so, from shadows to starlight, from silence to stories, I learned that imagination is not an escape—it is a key. A key to the doors we never dared to open, to the colors we never thought to name, to the dreams we never believed were ours to tell. And if you listen closely, in the quiet corners of your mind, you'll hear it too—the whisper of a story waiting to be dreamed into existence.*

# 14. Between Shadows & Starlights

In the hush of a library where lost souls weep,
I found voices buried, in silence deep.
Stories locked in dust-lined pages,
Echoes of dreams trapped through ages.
I wandered through the sleepless mind,
Seeking whispers fate left behind.
What if a color could change the past?
What if the darkest was not the last?
A shade beyond black, deeper than night,
Where sorrow melts into silent light.
Where broken hearts don't break in vain,
Where love is more than fleeting pain.
I traced the threads of the unspoken,
Words left unsaid, promises broken.
Time stood still in a breath once taken,
And love returned, though long forsaken.
I sat alone at a table for one,
Counting stars that had long been gone.
Ego had screamed, regret had stayed,
And silence spoke the words I never said.
Yet here I stand, between shadows and starlight,
In a world that was never just black and white.
For even the dark holds secrets untold,
And even the lost have stories of gold.

So if you find yourself in forgotten dreams,
In echoes, in shades, in quiet streams—
Know that somewhere, in the midnight hue,
There's a poem still waiting, just for you.

*"As the ink fades from these pages and the last verse finds its resting place, know that this story does not end here. Time is like a river—always flowing, always changing. And so are the stories we tell. Until we meet again, in the whispers of the winds or the stillness of the stars, may your heart continue to echo the worlds we have imagined."*

www.ingramcontent.com/pod-product-compliance
Lightning Source LLC
LaVergne TN
LVHW041237150826
845673LV00008B/2403

* 9 7 9 8 8 9 7 4 4 1 8 0 8 *